KICKING
Through Fields of Hope

By
South Gate High School Girls' Soccer Teams

Coordinated by
Luz Hernández-Hidalgo and José Hidalgo

Produced by

Strong Women

Jóvenes Escritores Latinos

Strong Women's Anthology
KICKING
Through Fields of Hope

Produced by

Luz Hernández-Hidalgo and José Hidalgo
Coordinators and editors
#JELSouthGate

All rights reserved to Strong Women
Non-profit organization - ID 831482997
StrongWomenCalifornia@gmail.com
www.strongwomenhtc.com

ISBN: 978-1-953207-71-5
Editorial #JEL - Jóvenes Escritores Latinos
Miriam Burbano, President
info@editorialjel.org
Impreso en USA

Dedication

This book is dedicated to all of those student-athletes that understand that they are able to accomplish anything they put their minds to as long as they are willing to put the work. To our girls' soccer team which understand that they are powerful women. To those young ladies which are yet to learn how powerful they are.

4

Acknowledgments

We want to thank all the student-athletes which took the time to share their stories and experiences. Jóvenes Escritores Latinos (JEL) for giving them a voice. Strong Women, a community non-profit organization which got us in contact with JEL as both focus on the youth and empowering them. Thank you to all the parents which are allowing our student-athletes at South Gate High School to express their thoughts. To Ms. Miriam Burbano which walked us through the process of putting this book together. Thank you for your patience and guidance. Ms. Luz Hernandez-Hidalgo for getting us in contact with Strong Women and introducing me to Women Empowerment and teaching me to believe in how awesome our girls are.

Description

This is book shows the challenges that high school female student-athletes face at times they do not receive the same recognition than their male peers that play sports receive. The following poems and essays were written not only by girl soccer players but also by cross-country and track and field female and male athletes who are willing to share their experiences on and off the field.

Prologue

This book started as an idea to have the ability to fundraise for the South Gate High School Girls' Soccer Team which won the Division III CIF Los Angeles City Championship. However, as we started the process and began to organize the essays and poems, we started to see that our student-athletes have something to say and what better way to give them a loud voice through a book. It is interesting to see how both male and female athletes saw inequalities between how female athletes are treated and seen. At the same time it is good to see that their voices will be heard beyond our city limits. I am thankful for this opportunity but most of all I am proud to be their teacher and coach.

Coauthors:

Brianna Bernal, Vanessa Sandoval, Allison Vianney, Leah Guzmán, Bernie Torres, Katherine Chica, Fabian Vasquez, Yadira Valadez, Leslie Cristales, Dalia Martínez, Giselle Ramirez, Antonio Sanchez, Montserrat Hidalgo, Darlene Mendoza, Esbeidy Recendiz, Maritza Cervantes, Valeria Serrano, Scarlett Gutierrez, Henry Tercero, Guadalupe Cacho, Cruz Rodriguez, Natalie Mejia, Andrea Flores, Lyzet Leyva, Lauren Villalta, Yoseline Panduro, Giselle Bustos, Denise Ramirez, Yoseline Martínez, Hector Huizar, and Sebastiana.

Coordinator Luz Hernández-Hidalgo

Helping working moms, career women, and entrepreneurs find a proactive way to empower their daughters in a fun and creative space. I lead girl empowerment workshops by creating an environment that inspires mindset growth; encourages taking risks in a compassionate way; and provides the freedom to communicate openly.

My vision is to empower girls with the tools they need to succeed in life. I want each girl to go after what they want without excuses, fears, or judgment from any challenges they may face. Instead they will experience resilience and persistence to reach their highest self everyday by choosing who they are first. These mindset shifts will heal them inside out. Nourishing the mind and body is an integral part of early development into their adult years.

Let's Empower Our Girls!

By Luz Hernández-Hidalgo

As a Girlife facilitator, coach, and speaker, I have heard the disempowering messages our girls get to hear constantly from social media, tv shows, society or even their parents.

When I work with the girls, we get to dismantle the disempowering messages they get to hear on a regular basis. Some examples in sports are: girls are emotional and weak; girls can't play sports; girls are dramatic; she must be acting up because she is in her time of the month. When speaking about how these messages make them feel, some girls express that it is funny because they know it's not true. Others feel upset to hear those disempowering messages.

It's tough! I know... As these disempowering messages are vital to a girl's social and emotional development, girls desire to play sports.

Sports give them a sense of belonging to a team where she feels included and accepted for the way she is, not based on her appearance the physical stigma plays a role in her success.

Establishing a sense of belonging starts at a young age when we create safe spaces for our girls to express themselves without being judged; where she feels confident about her uniqueness; being herself no matter what others think, this means belonging in her own skin.

Remember your daughter was born to "belong" not to fit in. Shattering those limiting beliefs (disempowering messages) starts at home when you support your daughter with unconditional love. Let her know that her uniqueness is more valuable than the standards society imposes on her to provide her with opportunities to play sports that she enjoys and where she can excel. She will then know that all she needs is to set her mind to extraordinary things.

Coordinador José Hidalgo

My name is José Hidalgo, I am originally from Guadalajara, Jalisco México. I came to the United States when I was eight years old. I started teaching in 2003 and came to South Gate High School in 2005. Luckily, I began to coach girls soccer at South Gate High in 2006 with my mentor Mr. Vaca. I have a wonderful, supportive wife and two outspoken daughters. I am proud and honored to be a teacher, soccer, cross country, and track and field coach. I enjoy reading and cooking. When I retire I want to be able to go to culinary school to continue developing my cooking skills.

Powerful Women

By José Hidalgo

Please do not judge them because you think that they do not belong on the soccer field.

On the contrary, many times anything guys can do, they can do it better.

Watch how determined they are, and how hard they are willing to work for what they want.

Energized, they are ready to practice rain or shine.

Respect is what they deserve.

Full with commitment they step into the soccer field.

Unfortunately their biggest critics are their own classmates and friends

Limiting their ideas of how successful these girls are, luckily they have proved them wrong.

Without a question, champions, they deserve to be.

Only themselves can stop them. Who are we to stop them or put that idea in their heads?

Men, you need to understand that these girls are our daughters, sisters, friends.

Enough with us trying to make them doubt.

Not my place to doubt them but instead to make them believe that they are "POWERFUL".

From the Desk of Christina Montalvo President of Strong Women

As the Strong Women President I feel it is my duty to identify and support our local youth groups. City of South Gate High School Girls Soccer Team won the CIF Championship for the 2nd year in a row. They were fundraising for their championship rings and we decided to step in and help with their efforts. Not only do these young women excel in sports but they also volunteer at community events, assist the local chapter of Kiwanis, and a couple are girl scouts. They all maintain above average grades in school.

It is vital that we support, motivate, and encourage these future leaders of tomorrow. As a part of the Strong Women mission we take pride in empowering young women. We wish them all the best in the next few years in their achievements and endeavors.

Please look for us and our upcoming projects that continue to heal our communities.

Facebook:
https://www.facebook.com/strongwomenhealing/
IG: @strongwomenhtc

#swhtc #strongwomen

Thank you for supporting Strong Women Healing Their Community and our youth.

From the Desk of Miriam Burbano
President of #JEL
Jóvenes Escritores Latinos

The purpose of #JEL is to motivate our youth to use letters as tools to bring justice and equality to our communities.

What a great honor it is to have the opportunity to know that the essays and poetry in this book bring attention to a problem in our society that should already be a part of our sad history; gender equality in all areas.

It is certainly painful to read Brianna Bernal´s lines telling us clearly how she feels about being a woman in sports:

"... inequality here
Inequality there...
And that's not all to mention
Working many hours and getting home late
To get a paycheck with no equal pay
We work hard to get appreciated…"

Once we get over that moment of pain reading these lines, we realize that our young women are strong enough to have the courage to express their feelings in writing, the fight continues and this issue is not forgotten. It fills us with power and motivation to know that we have young leaders who continue this fight against discrimination against women and demand respect for all.

#JEL has literary groups in six Latin American countries and in the United States motivating everyone to talk about the problems of their communities and tell their stories because if they don't do it, no one will do it for them.

In Colombia, young people write about overcoming youth depression and condemn domestic violence. In Guatemala they write about acts of kindness and love for grandparents. In El Salvador JEL writers talk about peace and technology while in Mexico they write about the talents we all have. Ecuador and Honduras are also present to write about the urgency of saving our planet and the problems that technology has brought us.

Thank you to the Los Angeles community for supporting #JEL and the youth writers of the South Gate High School Girls' Soccer Team that won the Division III CIF Los Angeles City Championship. Congratulations to everyone on the team!

facebook.com/JEL2014
info@editorialjel.org
jel2013.blogspot.com

Del Escritorio de Miriam Burbano
Presidente de #JEL
Jóvenes Escritores Latinos

El propósito de #JEL es motivar a nuestros jóvenes a utilizar las letras como herramientas para traer justicia e igualdad a nuestras comunidades.

Que gran honor es tener la oportunidad de saber que los ensayos y poesías de este libro trae la atención a un problema de nuestra sociedad que ya debería estar superado; la igualdad de géneros en todas las áreas.

Es ciertamente doloroso leer a Brianna Bernal cuando sus versos declaran claramente lo que siente al ser una mujer en los deportes:

"...Desigualdad aquí
Desigualdad ahí...
Y eso no es todo para mencionar
Trabajar muchas horas y llegar tarde a casa.
Para obtener un cheque de pago sin salario igual
Trabajamos duro para ser apreciados…"

Una vez que superamos ese momento de dolor al leer estas líneas, nos damos cuenta que nuestras jóvenes mujeres tienen el valor de expresar sus sentimientos por escrito, la lucha sigue y este tema no está olvidado. Nos llena de poder y motivación saber que tenemos líderes jóvenes que continúan con esta lucha en contra de la discriminación en contra de la mujer y demandan que se respete a todos sin importar su género.

#JEL tiene grupos literarios en seis países latinoamericanos y en los Estados Unidos motivando a todos a que hablen de los problemas de sus comunidades y cuenten sus historias porque si ellos no lo hacemos, nadie lo hará por ellos.

En Colombia los jóvenes escriben sobre la superación de la depresión juvenil y condenan la violencia doméstica. En Guatemala ellos escriben sobre los actos de bondad y el amor a los abuelitos. En El Salvador se escribe sobre la paz y la tecnología mientras que en México se escribe sobre los talentos que todos tenemos. Ecuador y Honduras también se hacen presentes para escribir sobre la urgencia de salvar nuestro planeta y los problemas que la tecnología nos ha traído.

Gracias a la comunidad angelina por apoyo a #JEL y a los escritores juveniles del equipo de fútbol femenino de South Gate High School que ganó el campeonato de la ciudad de Los Ángeles CIF de la División III. ¡Felicitaciones a todo el equipo!

facebook.com/JEL2014
info@editorialjel.org
jel2013.blogspot.com

South Gate High School Girls' Soccer Team Division III CIF Los Angeles City Champions

South Gate High School Girl's Team

Brianna Bernal

Hello, my name is Brianna Bernal. I am 15 years old and am a current sophomore. I am an athlete at South Gate High School. I participate in cross-country, soccer, and track & field. I had taken a break from soccer but got back in condition for my freshman year. I am a defender on the field and do long distance for track.

Women Inequality
By Brianna Bernal

Inequality here
Inequality there
Inequality's everywhere
From across the room
To around the world
There's no way to escape it, we can only hope
In all sort of activities like school or sports
Or in teeny tiny offices with no doors
Less money
Less attention
And that's not all to mention
Working many hours and getting home late
To getting a paycheck with no equal pay
We work hard to get appreciated
But instead we get deeply hated
Men say that we're useless
But really they're clueless.
They think we are weak
But can they even think?
They expect us to cook and clean
And then to treat them like kings
We can't catch a break
Or else they start to hate
We have to be careful with what we wear
Because men will stare
we turn into their prey when we walk alone
when an "inconvenience" happens first thing they ask is what
you wore
You'll feel very lonely and torn

South Gate High School Girl's Team

And after that you won't be able to do things you used to
adore
Nothing will ever be the same as before.
Inequality is worldwide
It's like they don't want women to thrive
In some places we can't drive
In the middle east wives can't divorce
so they stay with their spouse by force
It's sad to think that this isn't the worse
It's like being a female is a curse.
The men around tell us we have made progress
But when we speak of equality
We speak for the equality of every women
We speak for the young black girls
the young brown girls
the young indigenous girls
For they are the future women.

Vanessa Sandoval

My name is Vanessa Sandoval and I am a senior at South Gate High School. I will be attending Cornell University in Fall and studying Environmental Science. During my free time I enjoy participating in Varsity Cross-Country, Track and Field, and Student's Run LA. I also write short stories and poetry.

Women Empowerment
By Vanessa Sandoval

We live in a generation in which women are defined by the lengths of their skirts where if we are not conforming to standards our femininity is disvalued, where we are told we live in a country of equality, but at the dollar we are statistically of lower value, though we come from the very interior of the feminine figure.

There are threats to the right of our autonomy; there are still patriarchal powers that constrain us in our limits, but beyond these realities, there are hidden expectations, while we are craved and fantasized.

We are only ever respected if deemed of desire, we are seen as objects of fulfillment, as if there is anything we owe.

When I speak of women, I reference the figures who have shown there is more to life than submission to the "American" dream.

I reference the blood shed at the cost of the fight for justice, I reference the strength of mothers, and the simple existence of every women who stands today, and as long as we remain in the shackles of expected femininity.

As long as there is disparities amongst any women, then there is no equality in this society.

Allison Vianney

My name is Allison Vianney Olvera. I'm a senior at South Gate High School. I like to run, and I am a part of the school's track and cross country team. I am also a peer college counselor for students at my high school. I like to watch movies in my spare time.

Women Equality
By Allison Vianney

In the year 1920, women in the US were granted the right to vote. In 1803, the first academy for higher education was opened for women. These milestones were a step forward to equality in the US. With women being in the working force just as much as men are, and women having the rights of the US constitution applying to them, it would seem as if gender equality existed in our country. But in my opinion we aren't there yet.

One issue in our country that women face that shows gender inequality, is the right to control their own bodies. According to the online article, "Texas Abortion Restrictions" written by Erin Douglas and Carla Astudillo, under one of Texas abortion laws "anyone who performs or aids with the abortion can be sued — and by almost anyone". This takes away a person's right to bodily autonomy because the people who are denied an abortion will be forced to carry a child unwillingly.

Apart from being forced to carry a life, women are also being stripped of the ability to create it. Women in prisons and immigration detention facilities have been going under sterilization surgeries nonconsensually. Forced sterilization of women in prison stemmed from the idea of eugenics. Women were sterilized nonconsensually, legally in every state across the U.S., up until 1979. But this still is happening today. According to the article "Survivors of California's forced sterilizations", written by Erin McCormick, in 2001 Kelli Dillion had a surgery done in a women's facility as an inmate where, "surgeons had removed her ovaries during what was supposed to be an operation to take a biopsy and remove a cyst". Following her report of this, investigations found that several hundred inmates had been nonconsensually sterilized throughout the decade.

The right to bodily autonomy for women is still being contested in the U.S.. There are other problems women in the U.S. face like the wage gap that prove gender equality doesn't exist in our country.In other parts of the world, the right to vote, right to an education, and other rights aren't given to women. So in my opinion, across the world, gender equality still does not exist.

Some people think that gender equality is just giving women the right to vote, pursue an education, and get a job. But there are ways women are controlled by governments in ways men aren't. Apart from those, women are also degraded, disrespected, and judged because of their gender. It's difficult to imagine if the world will ever be truly gender equal.

Leah Guzmán

Hello, my name is Leah Guzman and I live in South Gate California. I am 16 years old and currently a junior. I play soccer and decided to also join the track and field team this year at South Gate High School. I recently just started getting into soccer sophomore year and enjoyed it, so ever since then I have tried to improve my skills to be a better player on the field. I also plan on majoring in interior designing after high school.

Women Empowerment

By Leah Guzmán

In our world today people often have that mindset or opinion that some things are only "for girls" and some things are only "for boys". Many times people allow others to tell them that they can not do something or participate in something because it's only for girls or it's only for boys.

Examples that have to do with this would be sports, jobs, and clothing. I feel like our population has a strong opinion on these things and think that some are only for girls and some are only for boys. In my opinion I believe that nothing is for only girls or only for boys because everyone deserves to be qualified to do anything they want.

Our population should not discriminate against a guy or a girl for participating or doing something that they think should only be for a girl or only for a boy because if that individual enjoys what they are doing then that is all that matters.

When it comes to sports some individuals think that certain sports can only be played by girls and some can only be played by boys. For instance, when it comes to football everyone thinks of it as only a boy sport and if a girl decides she wants to play football people will judge her and she will probably feel left out. Our population should not judge a girl for wanting to play football or any other sport that people think is only for guys. Every individual should be allowed to play whatever sport they want even when it comes to boys as well. For boys, some people think that cheerleading is only a sport for girls and if they see a boy in the cheer team they automatically start making assumptions about that boy.

I do not think it is fair to judge those girls or boys who want to try something new because no specific sport should be for only girls or boys, it should be for everyone. If a guy wants to be in the cheer team or a girl wants to join the football team we should not make them feel like they are being judged for something new they want to try out because what if that individual is passionate about that particular sport instead we should support them.

Another area where I feel our society has the same mindset about it only being for girls or only for boys is jobs. People tend to think that there are certain jobs specifically for girls or specifically for boys when that is not the case.

Every person should have that mentality that they can apply for any job and not have to second guess their choice because they think that it is only meant for a girl or only meant for a boy. An example of a job that I feel people think is only for boys is construction and a job people think is only for girls would be a fashion designer.

People tend to think that just because construction has to do with building things girls can not do it, but that should not matter because you never know what a girl is capable of doing until you see it for yourself. Now for fashion designers people automatically think that a girl can only design clothing and boys are incapable of doing that which is not true because boys are skilled as well to become a fashion designer.

Nevertheless no job should be examined as only for girls or only for boys because like I mentioned both genders are skilled to work in any profession they want, so we should not let our society have that frame of mind that certain jobs are for girls only or boys only.

Lastly, another area society seems to think of as only for girls or only for boys is clothing. Now I feel like this is a major area where individuals have this outlook because people consistently get judged for what they wear sometimes.

For instance, some clothing that people think is only indicated for boys are hats and certain jeans or shirts. Clothing that people think is only indicated for girls would be shirts like crop tops and skirts.

So, if someone saw a girl dress like a guy they would automatically judge her for wearing boy clothing and vice versa if a boy wore girl clothing. There should not be particular clothing for boys and for girls everyone should have the freedom to wear whatever they want and not have to be judged by it.

Our society should have the way of thinking that specific attires are not only meant for boys or only for girls, but implied to everyone.

In conclusion, I think there should not be certain things for only boys or only girls. All things should be for both genders; they should not feel like they are going to be judged by other individuals. Humanity has to have the mentality that everything is for both girls and boys like in the examples I mentioned sports, jobs, and clothing.

Even if you do not agree with everything being for boys and girls you should not let your opinion get in the way of what someone else thinks. Obviously not everyone is gonna see eye to eye with the outlook of others, but the best thing you could do is let them be themselves and have their own point of view on things.

This is why I think certain things should not be for only girls or only boys, it should be equal for both genders.

Bernie Torres

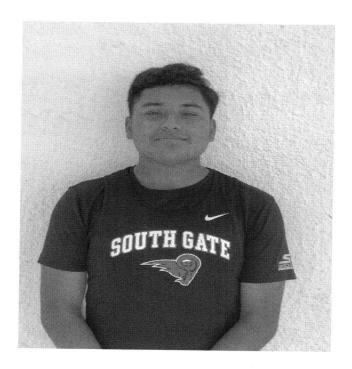

Hello my name is Bernie Torrez and I am currently a student attending South Gate Senior High. I consider myself active, go-getter, curious, and adventurous. I am currently in track and field and I focus on two events: the 1600m and shot put. I was also in Cross Country and in SRLA. I have been in Track and Field for 1 year, Cross Country for 3 years, and SRLA for 5 year. My favorite out of those 3 is SRLA. My fastest marathon is 4:01:38, my fastest mile is 5:23, and my furthest throw for Shot Put as of now 30'.1" feet.

Women's Empowerment
By Bernie Torres

Women's empowerment month is a month where we can celebrate and be thankful for all the powerful and beautiful females in the world. Why does our society decide that some things are just "for girls" or "for boys"? How does society choose which "jobs" or "tasks" are for boys or for girls? There are a couple of things that lead up to these decisions. Gender stereotypes and gender roles.

Extreme gender stereotypes are harmful because they don't allow people to fully express themselves and their emotions. For example, it's harmful to masculine folks to feel that they're not allowed to cry or express sensitive emotions.

Another example of stereotypes are that only girls can wear dresses and boys only wear suits. And it's harmful to feminine folks to feel that they're not allowed to be independent, smart or assertive. Breaking down gender stereotypes allows everyone to be their best selves whichever way it is.

Gender roles in society means how we're expected to act, speak, dress, groom, and conduct ourselves based upon our assigned sex. For example, girls and women are generally expected to dress in typically feminine ways and be polite, accommodating, and nurturing. Another example is that men do all the dirty work and are supposed to have a tough guy act no matter the situation they are in.

I think that society chooses what things are "for girls" and "for girls" because we cannot accept the fact that we are all equal. Society chooses what things are made for them by how they look and how they act. For example, society would assume me as a person who hits the gym a lot and who wouldn't care about others except myself. Society also chooses what things are for by their "Zodiac sign". Since I am a "Leo" I have compassion and big-heartedness, consciousness, drive, and natural leadership.

Women Empowerment is the process that creates power in women to live a happy and respectable life in a society. Women are empowered when they are able to access opportunities in a variety of fields such as in education, profession, lifestyle, etc., without any limitations and restrictions. It includes raising their status through education, awareness, literacy and training. It also includes the authority to make decisions.

When a woman makes a crucial decision, she feels empowered.

Katherine Chica

Hello my name is Katherine Chica I am 15 years old and I was born in Bellflower. I live in South Gate California and attend school at South Gate High School. I'm on the varsity soccer team and joined track and field this year. I also have played on the volleyball team and was on the cross country team as well. I love to travel. I've been to El Salvador, Paris, and Spain.

Society Gender Roles
By Katherine Chica

We live in a divided society where many people think it's ok to set gender roles for boys and girls because they think it's creating a safe space, while the other half strongly oppose and think setting gender roles is harmful to children.

I for one think setting gender roles on children is creating a dangerous and harmful environment. What children get told from an early stage stays with them forever. Children's minds are like clay, they can easily be told what to think and this sets the tone for the rest of their lives consciously and subconsciously.

To begin, we can go back to early childhood and start as simple as color. We are constantly told that pink is for girls and blue is for boys. This color gender role is engraved into the minds of children and creates an impactful imprint.

Color has no gender, but because some people in society believe that color reflects masculinity and femininity, it creates a burden for children to express themselves creatively. Now, young boys will fear choosing colors that are for "girls" such as pink or purple.

Likewise, the same burden can be placed on girls and can stop them from choosing "boy"colors such as blue or black. Aside from color, there are many other "gender-set" roles and expectations for boys and girls. Another one includes expressing our emotions. This "gender expectation" primarily targets boys.

There are many expressions and says stating "manly men don't cry", etc. There are some societies (like the Hispanic society) that believe men should not show their emotions because it makes them look weak.

This belief tremendously impacts boys both emotionally and mentally. As humans, we are programmed to feel emotions and shouldn't feel ashamed to do so. Neither should we get bullied or treated any different from others if we do.

Lastly, there are the gender roles that are played by members of the household. It is more common to see daughters and mothers do indoor cleaning, like washing the dishes and cooking meals. While sons and fathers are more commonly seen doing "the dirty work". This type of household gender role is influenced from a young age.

There are many kitchenette toys targeting little girls. You will typically see little girls on the packaging of their toys more than little boys.

Similarly, there are toys that only target little boys such as construction tools and "heavy-work" items which only promote boys on their packaging as well. All in all, both of these toys subconsciously train little kids from a young age that they have specific duties to take on once they get older.

To end, I think this type of mindset where boys and girls are told what and what not to do is dangerous and limits their capabilities.

Boys are allowed to express their emotions and take on the role of a chief in their household as equally as a girl. Likewise a young girl has the same right to take on "heavy-duty" roles within society. It's time to start thinking with fairness and allow children (and adults) to do what they desire.

Fabian Vasquez

My name is Fabian Vasquez, I was born in Los Angeles California in 2004. I live with both my brothers and two parents. I currently live in South Gate and I attend South Gate High school. Some of my extracurriculars include Cross-Country and Track & Field. My favorite subjects are Math, Health, and Spanish. I would describe myself as a determined, hardworking responsible individual. These characteristics are reflected in my school life but also in my personal life. One of the things that fascinate me the most are Trucks and Sports Cars. I am currently getting prepared for my college life and I hope to attend the University of California Irvine. I think it's a beautiful campus and I feel like I fit in.

Societies Gender Norms
Por: Fabian Vasquez

"Dresses are for girls and suits are for boys". We hear these comments from friends, family, peers, and on social media. Why is it that society has put these gender norms on us ever since we were little? What are the downsides of having to grow up with these constant norms? What can we do to change this? We need to take hold of our own lives.

We see changes in society's norms daily. From body positivity to female empowerment. These positive changes are creating ways for better norms in society.

Yet gender norms have seemed to stay the same. Seeing these norms left and right, only girls wear skirts, and only boys wear baggy pants. Scrolling through social media with daily reminders even if you don't notice them at first.

Seeing and hearing these norms throughout our lives can lead us to not show our true identity. Who are we if we follow everyone else? If we follow society's norms and don't make our own decisions, we are a copy of society. There are plenty of boundaries between genders as it is. These gender norms under our physical identity can limit us and take a mental impact as well.

Growing up with these norms keeps us on society´s leash, once we realize who we are we can break free and create our own ideals. Just like society's other norms, it's time we let go of these gender norms.

Not only for those who identify as females but also males. If there were to be a generation who grew up without these norms they would have a strong sense of self-expression.

A way to express themselves without society saying it doesn't correspond with their gender. It sounds incredible for a female to go out in a suit without society giving them the side-eye. A male going out with makeup on, without society telling them it's wrong. It's time we allow ourselves to express who we are without listening to society's do's and don'ts.

Society's gender norms are not creating a positive impact. They create boundaries between genders and self-expression. It's time to express ourselves in our own way. Without society's norms, and soon to be everyone's own identity. Goodbye to "guys only and girls only".

Yadira Valadez

My name is Yadira Valadez. I play Varsity soccer for South Gate High School. The position I play is defense. My birthday is June 15, 2006, I'm 15 years old, and a sophomore. This was my first year playing high school soccer and I also participated in Volleyball and Track Field.

Powerful Women
By Yadira Valadez

What is gender equality you might ask? It is actually a very important subject in our world today.

Gender equality is important because it gives fairness to everyone no matter what gender you identify by. Not only that but gender equality is essential for economic prosperity.

Societies that value women and men as equal are safer and healthier. Gender equality is a human right. Women are often perceived as less powerful or soft beside men. The argument is usually that men can do more than women, but the hard truth is otherwise women can do equal to what men can do and if not they can do much more.

Although we would like to believe gender equality is normal and should be in our society today, that is not always the case. I believe gender equality does not exist in all aspects of our country and world. There are many injustices involving gender in our world, for example equal pay. European countries have a more persistent pattern in the difference of wages.

As of 2021 the most recent figures place the average woman's earnings at around 80% of the average man's, though this varies significantly between occupations. This is statistically proven by the gender wage gap on wikipedia.

This makes me nervous for my future and makes me wonder how this has been happening for so long with no one being held accountable.Another issue in the work media is vacation time and work hours. 25 percent of women are forced to return to work within 2 weeks of giving birth to support their families. As shown on the website healthline.com.

Mothers are often able to go on maternity leave while fathers that have new babies need to continue working and are unable to bond with their newborn. They are able to care for a child just as much as a woman and should have the right to enjoy such a special moment. This all starts as we are kids and growing up with stereotypes, and what is and is not allowed for genders.

Growing up I feel like there were always labels preventing boys and girls to do what they'd like. Growing up pink was for girls and blue was for boys, most gender reveals use these colors till this day but I believe you can like whatever color you want.

You can do as you please and there should not be labels on things determining if they are for girls or boys.
Kids should be able to grow up with the freedom of making these decisions for themselves and should not have to follow a certain stereotype where specific toys, colors or clothes are not allowed simply because of gender.

I also believe parents should not give their input or pressure their kids to do what they want. But should support and be happy their kids are able to make their own choices. It is harmful to kids to have them grow up believing the labels and make them close minded.

They can get confused and be afraid to be themselves, they are our future and we should help our future generations grow into better people where everyone is accepted no matter the differences.

I have done things that are outside of the norm for my gender and I feel like nowadays it is normal and many people have done this.

As a girl growing up most of us played with barbies or dress up and etc because that's what we were taught. While boys played sports and played with toy cars.

I didn't play sports growing up but I was always very drawn to them. Now that it is my choice I play soccer, volleyball and track. Sports that are often male dominated, especially soccer. In soccer there are many things that may not be "ladylike".

For example, sliding in mud and getting dirty to win the ball. Being tough and bodying others to gain control over the game, excessively sweating and running for the love of the game. Just because I play does not make me any less of a lady and I'd like to think our generation now agrees with me and believes women can do anything men can.

Men and women are powerful and equal. Nobody should be treated differently or feel unaccepted because of gender. There should be no stereotypes or titles on things we do. Regardless of gender we are all human with weaknesses and strengths in all aspects of life. Gender equality helps us live in harmony and is important because it is justice for all.

Leslie Cristales

Hi, my name is Leslie Cristales. I am 15 and I am a sophomore soccer athlete from South Gate High School. My positions on the field are midfielder and defender. I used to play soccer back when I was eight for AYSO but then stopped. When I first came to the high school after quarantine I had decided to go back to it. I really liked going against others and how soccer would bring out the inner me. I also have decided to play the last 2 years of high school and then from there continue in college as a side hobby.

Powerful Women
By Leslie Cristales.

Most of the time people always have opinions towards what is "only for girls" or what is "only for boys".

This topic is very popular in our generation now because everybody wants to do everything. Doesn't matter if it's only for girls or boys. I believe that both girls and boys can do whatever they want no matter if it's only called out for a specific gender. People believe that certain things that guys do shouldn't be done by girls because they wouldn't be good enough or meet the requirements like a boy. An example is sports. People say sports are only for boys and aren't really for girls but in reality girls have the strength and power to do any sport they want. As for boys, they can't dress up as girls because they aren't considered girls.

An example would be LGBTQ + because there are guys who get called out or bullied for doing things that only girls do. For instance, getting your nails done, dressing up as a girl, putting wigs on, etc.

This topic also connects with kids and how they were taught to wear things or play with toys that are for their gender. It is very important that people realize that not everything should be considered for one gender and it should be for both.

Guys point out that girls aren't "strong enough" or how they are too "weak" to be in sports. Although, we do have the power to participate in sports. A great example is myself. I play soccer and I really enjoy playing it because I like to be active. Not only that but because I get to bring out the strength I have and put it on the field. Throughout the experience of playing soccer and playing against others who have been stronger than me shows that girls do have the power to be in sports. It doesn't matter if you're a boy or girl, everyone has the ability to play whatever they want and build from it.

I think we shouldn't get put down by other people just because we are girls. That has nothing to do with it because we were born to try new things no matter the gender.

Some people are against LGBTQ + and how most guys try to dress like girls and act like girls, even though they're not one. Things that girls do, anyone should be able to do it even if you aren't one yourself. I believe it's the person's opinion and decision to decide whether they want to do certain types of things or not. The reason I'm bringing LGBTQ + to this topic is because it relates to how some people don't like the fact that there are some guys who make themselves look like a girl.

In our generation, girls wear guy clothes and don't get pointed out for that but guys wearing girl clothes is a problem. People tend to ostracize the boy more for doing girly things. Although I still believe that nobody should be called out for something they want to do or enjoy doing.

As kids we were always taught to wear our appropriate gender clothes and play with toys that are for our gender. In my opinion, kids should be able to play with whatever they want and wear what they want. We should support kids and not tell them that certain things are "only for girls" or "only for boys". It will allow them to be who they want to be and put themselves out there. Parents shouldn't be stopping their kids from expressing how they are. People think that pink is for girls and blue is for boys but it shouldn't be put out like that. Sometimes girls like blue and boys like pink and people should accept that.

There should be no saying on what is "only for girls" or what is "only for boys". It should be the person's choice to do whatever they want to do. I, myself, love doing things that are known only for guys and it doesn't really matter. The reason for that is because I am the only one who gets to decide whether I want to do something or not. In the end we are human beings who get to play, wear, do, try new things and experience, and have our own voice no matter the gender. Therefore, our generation shouldn't define whether certain colors or activities are for a specific gender.

Dalia Martínez Zambrano

Dalia was born on August 22, 2005. She grew up in the city of Watts and later moved to South Gate, with her parents and younger sister, at the age of 12. Dalia is known to be outgoing, kind, hardworking, and determined. Some of her hobbies include cross country, soccer, track, and skateboarding. She also spends a lot of her time listening to music and drawing. A career that Dalia would like to pursue is in the medical field as a Registered Nurse.

Outside the Gender Norm
By Dalia Martínez

Growing up we are often told what we should and shouldn't do because it's considered our gender norms. Growing up, girls are told to play with dolls and boys with cars just because of their gender, not because of interest. Once either gender explores and enjoys a hobby or activity that is "outside gender norms," they get shamed upon with " you shouldn't do that because you are a girl/boy." or " only girls/boys do that." I'm sure we have all experienced this kind of stereotype throughout our lives.

I like to consider myself as a person who enjoys many physical activities like soccer and running. I've always had people around me who would support me and motivate me, up until I found a hobby that made my heart jump, which was skateboarding.

Skateboarding is a hobby that's been around for so many years, it continues to be a staple for many young kids to adults around the world. However, it is often overlooked as something that's, " only for boys."

At a young age, I would see many people skateboarding during the summer, including my own cousins. It's always looked interesting, all the tricks you can do, the way your board just sticks to your feet, it has always been beautiful to look at. When I was 14, on March 12,2020, Covid-19 hit the U.S. and hard. Everyone had to spend time in quarantine, but I took this as an opportunity to pursue something that has interested me for years.

I was able to learn tricks and was comfortable riding my board. I was so comfortable I decided to bring my skateboard everywhere I would go.

Initially, my family didn't take it so well. I received a lot of criticism and comments that skating is just for boys, or they all began making assumptions that maybe it was a way of me "coming out".

This was not the case at all, it was simply a hobby that made me happy. Riding on the skateboard on smooth pavement makes you feel like you're floating. Nothing compares to the satisfaction and excitement of landing a trick you've been practicing for hours or maybe even months on.

It was the first time that my family didn't support me. Despite all their efforts, I continued skating.

I influenced my other cousins, who were females, to get into skating and they also enjoyed it. My family didn't like this idea very much as it was unladylike.
My cousins, Miguel and Nataly, became like my brothers and sisters as our bond grew closer since we would all skate together. As weeks went by we all decided to try and explore local skateparks to continue to learn new things. The first park we attended was Wilson Skatepark located in Compton. Nataly and I were so nervous because we didn't know what to expect from the environment or the people.

Arriving, Miguel was able to make friends so easily, compared to Nataly and I. We were the only girls at the park, everyone kept giving us confused looks as if we didn't belong or if we were lost. The anxiousness and anxiety made our stomachs turn, but we continued doing what we knew how to do best, and that was to skate.

As the people around the park noticed us skating and our tricks, they became friendly and welcomed us into their community. Months went by and the people from the park ended up being our best friends.

The guys there helped Nataly and I with tricks and made sure we were safe. Nataly also noticed we also became an influence to other girls as more girls began to show up overtime.

It was truly an amazing experience but it had a bumpy start. I decided to continue because it was something that made me happy. It was very upsetting to see how many people tried to gate keep skateboarding for "just boys."

I believe any hobby should be open to everyone to experience and it isn't fair to be given restrictions just because of your gender. I felt relieved once I decided to keep pushing through the limits society and others have put on activities, clothing, makeup, etc. Skateboarding has made me more understanding and caring towards others. When skateboarding you meet people from different cultures or backgrounds. It has opened up a new world of style and self expression. This has made me feel a lot more comfortable in my own skin. I am glad I didn't let the expectations of society limit my experiences.

In short, gender norms shouldn't be a set back keeping you away from wonderful experiences. Like all other experiences, we learn and grow from them. It is important that we always remember what makes us happy and feel good about ourselves when making a decision. For example, I put myself and my happiness first when I decided I wanted to continue skating, and I hope others do the same. Your gender shouldn't be a factor that stops you from achieving your goals. At the end of the day, you will be doing something you enjoy rather than feeling regret. You only live once which is why it's best to make the most of it.

Giselle Ramirez

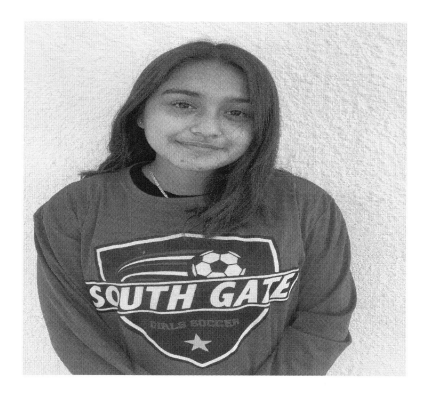

My name is Giselle Ramirez. I am 15 years old and I live in the city of South Gate, California. I attend South Gate High school and I play soccer and I am also part of Track and Field. I was a J.V. player in the first year of being on the team and little by little I became a varsity player. I love playing soccer. Playing soccer is like having therapy. It releases all my stress and my anxiety.

Only for Girls and Only for Boys

By Giselle Ramirez

I do not think all things have to be for boys or all things have to be for girls. For example, if a boy wants to wear a skirt he could because he likes it. Doesn't matter he's a boy he could wear whatever he wants. If a girl wants to wear a guy's boxers or guy's shirt or pants she could because she wants to. People have the right to do whatever they want and be who they want to become as long as they are respecting and not judging others. Even if it doesn't make other people happy.

I know that this does not always happen because for example, when a teacher needs help with something heavy they would normally ask a boy for help because they think a girl can't lift something that's heavy. The thought that certain sports are only for certain people. Football is for boys however, tennis is for girls. Girls should stick to certain sports like volleyball because soccer is an aggressive sport.

Girls could do anything a guy could do. I experienced this one time when I went to the park with my cousin. When we arrived there were some people there and as my cousin and I were getting ready to play soccer, I overheard one of the guys tell one of his friends "I am sure that she doesn't even know how to kick the ball or at least that is how she looks".

When I heard this, I was upset with the fact that someone was judging my soccer skills simply because I was a girl.

I do believe that people shouldn't judge people when you don't even know them because they could really surprise you. Clearly, the boys did not know that I have experience playing soccer and that I do have an idea on how to kick a ball and even to an extent know how to juggle a soccer ball.

As I continue thinking about how people are judged just because of their gender, I know that this is way more than a blue color that has to be for a boy or a pink color being for a girl.

Boys and girls should be able to participate in any sport they choose to do so because they like it and not because they are to participate in certain sports. Colors and even clothes are to be gender neutral but most importantly we can't continue to judge others without knowing them.

We have to respect and acknowledge those people that are different or stand out because of their beliefs or the choices they make when it comes to the things they like because different does not have to be bad but instead it can be unique.

Antonio Sanchez

Hello my name is Antonio Sanchez. I am currently a senior attending South Gate High School. The two sports that I have done for the last four years are Cross Country and Track & Field. My two favorite hobbies currently are running and watching anime.

Only for Boys, Only for Girls
By Antonio Sanchez

The idea that some things are only "for girls" or "for boys" has been around for a very long time. Throughout my lifetime I have always heard that there are things only meant for boys and for girls. I have always questioned who came up with this idea, and why has it been going on for so long.

Personally, I do not agree with some things only being meant "for girls" or "for boys" simply through my own experience, what I see in school, and around the world. During my adolescent years, I was always told by my parents that school is for girls because girls are smarter than boys. I honestly have no clue how I came up with this idea, but I believe I came up with this after comparing myself to some of the girls in the classroom. They would always get answers right, write nice, have good reading scores, and I was the complete opposite.

Their reaction was way different than what I anticipated. They told me that it is not true, and that school is for everyone and not just for girls.

Their advice to me was to try in school, and I would be as good as them. They were right because now I am in high school doing well and right on track to graduate. In high school I have recently noticed that many students are breaking the norm. By this I mean that there are boys who do things that are apparently only meant for girls and girls doing things that are only meant for boys. In my eyes I see students who are comfortable with breaking the norm, and truly expressing themselves.

I agree with what they are doing because no one should tell them that they can't dress or act a certain way based on some old idea. Even though I don't express myself like they do, I believe that this idea was some type of restriction for them to express themselves because they felt like they were going to be judged. However, they were brave enough to not care about being judged by the outside world and truly be free. Nowadays the idea of things being only for boys or girls is slowly starting to change.

As we may all know, Barbies have always been considered as a little girls toy, and legos would be considered as a boys toy. Now, there are going to be stores that don't specify if the toy is a girl or boy toy, and instead just has it as toys for everyone. I believe that is a big impact because little kids should be able to play with whatever toy they want to play with. No kid shouldn't be allowed to play with a toy because it is mainly played with by the opposite gender. As humans we are going through changes, and we have to disregard the idea that prevents people from breaking the norm.

To conclude, it is time for change. There shouldn't be this idea of certain things only being meant for girls or for boys. Every person should be allowed to do whatever makes them feel comfortable and allows them to express themselves fully. We are now living in a world where the norms are being broken, and we should see this as a normal thing. Once again, I do not agree with some things only being meant "for boys" or "for girls".

Kicking

Montserrat Hidalgo

I am Montserrat Hidalgo, a current 10th grader at South Gate Senior High School. I participate in sports such as Varsity Tennis, Varsity Soccer, Track and Field, and Cross Country. I enjoy reading, writing poems, and running. I like to think of myself as kind, friendly, honest, and a leader.

Only Boys

By Montserrat Hidalgo.

Every girl has heard those two words
The two words I wished they wouldn't have to hear
I wished I never heard
The words that hold us back
The ones that make us doubt
"Only boys"
They hold us back in chains
Society on the other end
Holding us where they think we should stay
We cry and weep for the chains to be broken
So that we can grow and bloom
It takes a while to find that we had the pliers all along
Only society told us we did not
Every day we search
Looking everywhere
We long for nurture
Yet every time we hear those words
Back to where you started
The never-ending cycle
End the cycle
Find the pliers
Show them "boys and girls"

Darlene Mendoza

My name is Darlene Mendoza, I am a senior attending South Gate High School. I am currently 17 years old and in both cross country and the track and field teams. I am not only a young woman of color but also part of the next generation of women changing the definition of what it means to be a WOMAN in today's society.

Oh to be a Woman

Por: Darlene Mendoza

A girl plays with dolls… I got dolls as a child. I can't remember the first time I got one, but every year since then I've gotten a doll up until I was maybe twelve. A boy plays with everything else from toys to girls' hearts…

My brother, he always got toy cars and nerf guns which seemed way cooler than a plastic doll that just sat and stared off into space, as if she was contemplating a life she could've lived beyond this role of a "perfect lady".

Nonetheless, I played with those dolls. I was told that dresses, dolls, and pretty little things were meant for girls becoming-woman and not boys destined to be men.

Soon these dolls turned into makeup, nail polish, perfume and purses. But! I don't like purses, I never have. I hate the smell of nail polish mixed with perfume, and worse of all makeup…

It's so hard and heavy, no one ever asked me if I wanted these things because if they had they would've known that little darling wanted cool jackets, and guns, and most of all I still wanted to play with toys.

I couldn't have these things… because I had to grow up faster than boys. I had to mature, it was decided when I had to grow up. And how… At this time I began to feel annoyed and frustrated with the idea of being a "WoMaN", simply because it wasn't fair. I didn't choose to be born a girl destined for womanhood, but I was.

This eventually led to me alienating myself from my body. I thought I was worth being a boy soon to be a man. I thought boys carried more value than girls.

Puberty started, and so did my body dysmorphia, I hated it but not because of what it looked like. But because I hated the idea of yet another uncontrollable factor in my life deciding who I'm to be in society....

I wanted to decide if I liked dolls or not and if I could get dirty or not. I felt trapped in my own head, as if I was watching everyone guide me into a life I couldn't walk away from... Just like some stupid doll stuck in some stupid trance. ...

But! I'm not some doll! I'm a young woman who's just as valuable and powerful as the man sitting next to me. I'm a woman who likes cars not carriages, tennis shoes not slippers, I like dresses too, but also oversized clothes meant to be worn by men. I can like things meant for men and still be a woman.

Esbeidy Recendiz

Esbeidy Recendiz was born on March 3rd in a small town in Reno Nevada. She now lives with her mom and siblings in South Gate, California. She currently is a Junior at South Gate High School. Her favorite subjects are physiology and biology. Esbeidy values herself as an honest, silly, hardworking, and driven person. She likes to use art as a form of expression which has led her to favor drawing and painting. Her hobbies include running, watching movies, listening to music, drawing, and going on adventures outdoors. Esbeidy wants to graduate high school and go to college; she wants to major in psychology and minor in criminology. She has always wanted to help people in a way and has become fascinated by the functions and structure of the human mind as well as the behaviors.

An Ode to Women

By Esbeidy Recendiz

Women's history month is one month where we actually acknowledge and celebrate women and their achievements.

Society downgraded women so low that we had to push for a month dedicated to just us, to us powerful women to us women who've fought who've perceived years and years of continuance oppression and in 1987 was when we formally celebrated.

No, we don't just dedicate one month, we dedicate each and every single day, from the wake of dawn to the set of the sun we celebrate our past, our present our future, we celebrate us Our sisters our mothers our daughters we celebrate, we rise above the hate and stereotypes that surround us we rise above and beyond.

We wake each day with a foot out ready to conquer and create, because we can, because we will, because we did we are extraordinary, we are fierce, we are unforgettable, we are women.

-Esbeidy Recendiz

Maritza Cervantes

Maritza Cervantes was born in the year 2005. She lives in Los Angeles with her parents and five siblings. She also attends South Gate High School, and plays for their soccer team. Her hobbies are playing soccer, of course, painting, and drawing. She likes going out to take walks on the beach. Especially listening to music, it keeps her at ease.

Gender Labels
Por: Maritza Cervantes

Gender labeling has become such a big issue in today's society. Gender norms often limit what girls and boys "can" and "can't" do. They label things,"only for girls" or "only for boys." Society has these labels normalized, which does not let us express ourselves freely without any judgment, or feeling self conscious. For example, when guys are open to expressing their feelings. Often people would invalidate their feelings by making it "known" that getting emotional is "just for girls". Even when girls sit a certain way, because it's not "lady-like". People are labeled throughout their whole life based on their physical appearance, how they act, or even because they just don't "fit in" society's image of men and women.

Society expects men and women to look up to their standards. Often women are more "feminine", and men are more "masculine". When girls are open to wearing anything that isn't pinky or glittery, they refer to them as "tomboys". Even when they want to look or be as strong as men. They will apparently look "big" and "bulky". Then building muscle should only "be for men". As well as when they play sports, or even when they just like to hang around with boys simply because they have the same interests. As for boys, when they play with Barbie's at a young age, they would say "put that down, it's for girls". As well as when they like to paint their nails, or open to wearing makeup. Most people would automatically assume they are gay. When should a piece of clothing, or an object determine what specific gender it belongs to? Everyone should use or wear whatever they want without society degrading them because of their gender.

The way society sets standards of how men and women should act is quite questionable. Women are often "overly emotional". It's true, yes, women are more likely to show emotion, but that's because society hardly allows men to express their feelings. As they would say "you're a man, don't cry" which simply feeling an emotion or just having a vulnerable moment , should not make them any less of their gender. As well as when girls sit a certain way, or even burp, but obviously say excuse me. Apparently it's "not lady-like". Girls are expected to always act accordingly, but men are not? The way we act, or feel, should not determine what gender it falls into.

Many of us have trouble trying to "fit in" society's image of men and women. They have many high standards of each gender's appearance. As stated before, men are to look more masculine, and women are to look more feminine. Truthfully, social media plays a big role in that. Women are expected to have a perfect body, but whenever girls don't match those standards people insult them. The term "having a little boy body" is so insulting to both genders. Even for men, they are expected to look nice and muscular. They are influenced by the media to look that way, and feel they have to live up to those standards. Kids should not be expected to be developed at such a young age. It sets unnecessary expectations of what each gender should look like.

Gender labeling plays a huge role in today's society. It generalized what specific behaviors should come from women and men. In reality what men, women, boys, and girls do, wear, act, look, should not be entitled to a specific gender. Society should not look up to those expectations, and let them express themselves freely. Let them be confident and comfortable in their own skin. There's no such thing as "for boys only" or "for girls only", it only exists if you let it. Be you.

Valeria Serrano

My name is Valeria Serrano. I was born on February 7th, 2006. I attend South Gate Senior High. I play Varsity high school soccer as well as club soccer for FC Premier. I like giving back to my community so I decided to join Key Club my freshman year and I am now serving as club President. I enjoy watching baseball games with my family and playing Roblox in my free time.

Gender Equality
By Valeria Serrano

What does gender equality mean? Gender equality impacts everyone's life on a daily basis. Gender is the way someone differentiates themselves in society. For example, one's norms, behaviors and roles. Equality is the state of having rights and opportunities. In other words, fairness and freedom. All humans should have the choice of behavior, dressing, and sports. Gender should not be described as stereotypes in society.

Firstly, all humans should have a choice of behavior. Women, men and others should be seen and given the same strengths. By economically participating in jobs, women should not be judged for being a construction worker. Likewise men should not be judged for being a hairstylist. Whether society says otherwise, all have the right to make choices of what they want to achieve.

Second, all humans should have a choice of dress. Clothing does not determine one's gender. Many people may think seeing a woman with a buzz cut is strange and likewise seeing a man with a dress is strange. It shouldn't be, society should see everyone the same whether the style belongs to a certain gender.

Lastly, all humans should have a choice of sports. In high schools many males participate in cheerleading. Over time people started to normalize this. From my personal experience, I've never seen a girl in a field with a crowd of boys playing football. It takes a lot of courage because of what society will say. Here, in South Gate Senior High we have a 9th grader participating in football which is one step closer to normalizing women and men in certain sports. No sport is just for women and no sport is just for men. Sports do not represent gender.

In conclusion, there should not be stereotypes to represent who a person really is. Stereotypes should not represent your gender or sexuality. Whether one is men or women or other society should not indicate certain behaviors, dress, or sport. There should be a change in where no one is judged by who they are or who they are becoming. All humans should have the choice of behavior, dress, and sports.

Scarlett Gutierrez

Hello my name is Scarlett Gutierrez. I was born July 6th 2006. I have 2 siblings, a brother and a sister, Samantha and Sammy. I'm Mexican-American and Filipino. My favorite foods are Filipino, Mexican, and American foods. I enjoy eating fried bananas, pozole, and wings. I attend South Gate High School where I play on the girls' soccer team. I've been captain of the varsity team since my freshman year and am still going strong. In the off season I play for my soccer club FC Premier. Soccer is one of my favorite hobbies.

South Gate High School Girl's Team

Gender Equality
By Scarlett Gutierrez

Gender equality, also know as sexual equality or equality of the sexes, is the state of equal ase of access to resources and opportunites no matter what gender you are. So in this case I do not believe gender equality exists in my school.

It sucks that my girls soccer team does not get the same treatment as football. So much gear and equipment is given to them. For example, they got a whole water station for practices and games. I wouldn't have a problem if we get that, but no, we have to bring our own water bottles. Recently, my team went to the playoffs and won the CIF Division III Championship. We got so much attention afterwards only because of that reason. Now on the other hand, boys teams get so much attention even if they don't win. My soccer team needs to raise money for our championship rings that we earned, who knows if the boys team would need to raise the money like us.

To stand out and make a difference you need to be known right? Yes, people tend to turn their backs on girl role models. When a girl finally steps up to the plate and tries to make a difference I hear things like, "She's boring. She is no fun". It's odd how once a boy steps up everyone agrees with him. It seems it's only because of his gender.

One of the lamest ways to show guys have an advantage over girls is to get dress coded. How come it's fair for a guy to wear a tank top but for a girl it's an "issue". I strongly disagree with the dress code because one time I got a dress code for showing a little bit of skin and I was told to zip up. One of my guy friends once told me he doesn't even care about it because nobody pays attention to what he wears. That tells me they only care about **what girls wear**.

There should be no difference between the male and female species, We are all the same no matter how big the norms or roles are. We can all be challenged the same by them. Maybe this inconvenience will end soon.

Henry Tercero

My name is Henry Tercero. I am currently a senior attending South Gate High School. I participate in sports such as Cross Country, Track and Field, and SRLA. I enjoy being active and going outside to venture out.

Gender Equality
By Henry Tercero

In this great Nation of Freedom and Equilibrium
There is showing of equality between man and women
Although many will say there is a great division
Forgetting the times of great opposition

The times of great gatherings and reunions
To disperse this disproportion
Roared across like wildfire
Which engulfed the nation into uniformity

Many show little interest to other Nations
Shackled and bound by old customs
Engulfed by their own illusion
Of still being oppressed

Women in varied nation
Engulfed and choked of the thought of change
Shackled And fastened into inferiority
Viewed and placed into presumed norms

Many had seen and felt the divergence
Which allowed and ensued a shift
Into the beliefs of many
Into the equality of both men and women

Guadalupe Cacho

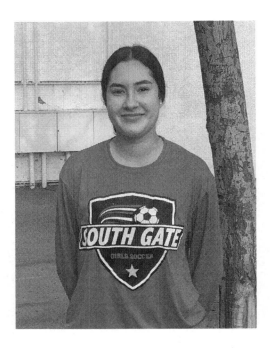

My name is Guadalupe Cacho Soto and I am 16 years old. I live in the city of South Gate and I attend South Gate High School. I live with both my parents and my two siblings. I started playing soccer when I was 9 years old and last year I joined the girl's soccer team at school. Last year, I participated in cross country and it was a great experience.

Gender Equality
By Guadalupe Cacho

Everyone has the right to live his/her life without discrimination. People of all genders should have equal rights, responsibilities, and opportunities despite their gender, culture, or color. Gender equality can only be achieved when both female and male individuals are treated similarly.

Gender equality is important because it helps prevent violence, especially against women and girls. It prevents violence against women by challenging stereotypes that give men power over women. For instance, men are usually always seen as the most powerful, violent person and women as the less powerful, abused person. Gender equality gives women the freedom they need to be themselves and leads them to healthier lives. Without gender, equality females are exposed to violence and discrimination which leads to anxiety, depression, and low self-esteem. This is so important because these factors can eventually lead to suicide. It is not right that women are usually silenced and aren't allowed to speak their minds/or express themselves. Everyone deserves to be able to use their voice as a weapon, especially women.

Gender inequality can be seen in various ways including in sports. That comes mainly in professional sports, where in almost all cases, men make more money than women. Stereotypes are often brought up when it comes to gender equality in sports. For example, males are more likely to participate in masculine sports than females while females are more likely to participate in feminine sports than males. I think females have the same ability and right to participate in masculine sports and males have the same ability and right to participate in feminine sports. These stereotypes are harmful because they make women feel less than who they are and this can also lead to women feeling less motivated to achieve their athletic goals and dreams. Girls like myself can often be discouraged when it comes to participating in sports in school for instance because we are so used to hearing sports are for boys and girls should focus on doing feminine things. Gender equality allows both females and males to participate in any sport they wish to participate in.

Gender equality is very important when it comes to education because it promotes fairness in education, as well as challenging stereotypes that have limited a student's potential. Gender equality will allow all students to be free to pursue their education without the fear of discrimination or harassment because of their gender.

Gender inequality is a big problem in education because girls face discrimination and stereotyping by teachers. Females are limited to certain education opportunities due to pregnancy or early marriage. Gender inequality affects schools because some teachers are poorly trained which gives students a disadvantage because they are not given the appropriate resources that would benefit their education needs. Overall, gender equality is important for both females and males but it affects females more. It helps prevent violence against women and it allows equal treatment and the same opportunities in sports. Gender equality is also an important factor in education and schools. Gender equality leads to a healthy and united society.

Cruz Rodriguez

My name is Cruz Rodriguez, I have two younger brothers. I am currently a senior attending South Gate High school. I've done cross country and track & field all four years. I was part of academic decathlon and I am also part of the journalism staff. I am hopeful for what's to come.

Gender Equality
By Cruz Rodriguez

The scales, they're not right
Always trying to hide that one big fight
As the world quakes and shakes
And the high chair unscathed, they are enjoying a latte.
Ignoring the fact that many are scared of facing the world
that they create
Until the uproar brings in a storm
Chaos ensued all just till it's their name
Just as there is a money game Many seem to play
Cheated and demeaned.
Just for once wanting civility
The scales in their favor are what is feared
The scale in balance is the dream
Yet there is no beam to shine
Keep in mind.
Times have changed improved
Yet we are not, the same
It is feared because it is new
New things are always feared
Until everyone starts to get used to it
Then and only then the scales will be right.

Natalie Mejia

Hi, my name is Natalie Mejia. I am 15 years old and I'm a sophomore at South Gate High School. I am a JV player for the girls soccer team and this is my first year playing this sport for South Gate High School. The person who motivated me to play soccer was my grandpa. Therefore I started playing for AYSO when I was 10 years old. Then I decided to play it again in high school and I really enjoyed the experience of being part of the team and playing against others.

Gender and Equality
By Natalie Mejia

Inequality is unspoken of at South Gate High School,
Let's not act like fools.
Students do this because they think it's cool,
Is it really cool calling someone names?
Calling a guy gay for doing cheer,
This is sad to hear.
In volleyball and tennis guys get shorts,
While girls get short skirts and spandex.
Is there seriously a reason for it all?
They doubt that a women is strong if she plays football,
They doubt she can't take it all.
They think she can't even catch a ball,
But when she's on the field she brings it on.
In soccer they watch boys play and only focus on the winner,
As for girls, they look at their figures.
Day to day guys get praised,
But with girls they don't even bother to watch our games,
Instead they call us names.
We overcame thoughts and beliefs,
Simply by winning a championship game.
With commitment and hard work everything is possible,
Just take the "Im" from impossible.
Now you know that we do make things possible.

Andrea Flores

Andrea Flores is a 14-year-old teenager who is currently enrolled in high school as a freshman. She is friendly and kind, but can also be lazy and shy or maybe she's just nervous. She was born in August 2007. She goes to South Gate High School and she enjoys playing her favorite sport soccer. She is very chill, brave and courteous. She loves losing to music, loves watching tv shows, movies, and she also loves her family

Anything for Anyone
By Andrea Flores

Our society decides what things are for boys and what things are for girls. I believe that anyone should get to choose what they want based on who they are not what they are. I am a girl and I enjoy playing soccer as much as the boys. And it could be many other things. Our society can decide what things are for people but people won't care. I don't think our society should decide which things are for boys or girls.

People shouldn't get to decide what you get based on your gender. You, yourself should get to choose what you want. It doesn't matter if it has a certain label of color or the way it's styled. Our society should decide which job or career we choose for our future. The government has more men working for them than women. It's crazy that a woman working for the government had become a Vice President for the very first time. It's something historical.

Nowadays our society has changed more and more. Back then women were judged more than men since women didn't have many rights. There have been many events in the history of gender equality of women facing discrimination. Nowadays women wear men's clothes and dress up. While men use different gender clothes and look very different. Our society has changed, many people have judged men for wearing different gender clothes even though they very much feel comfortable and feel at their very full potential.

Since the minute we were born we are given a color depending on what gender we are. The color pink defines a girl, and blue defines a boy. When we're young our parents decide what we get not knowing their things for a certain type of gender. As we grow older in life and develop who we are as a person. We now know what it means. Like if we like this or that or, if we like him or her. As we become more mature and expand we now get to decide which things are for us.

Gender equality is a good thing. Each individual can be equally powerful as should. But many people don't want it that way. Overall in gender equality women and men need to be treated the same with dignity, respect and fairness. Women and men need to be given the same resources, and opportunities. Each and every one of us should get to decide which things we want.

Lyzet Leyva

Lyzet Leyva was born in November of 2006, she lives with her parents and siblings in the city of South Gate, California. She attends South Gate Senior High. People would describe her as a loyal, honest, and intelligent young woman. Her favorite hobbies include playing soccer, volleyball, running, painting, listening to music, hanging out with her friends and family, especially her dogs. When she grows up she would like to attend a 4 year university where she will study to become a lawyer.

Equality

By Lyzet Leyva

Equality means to be equal
But we are nowhere even close to being equal
Although we have made some progress
It is not enough

Women are to be ladylike and proper
Men are to be manly and brave
Women must stay home and clean
Men must go to work and make money

As children girls play with dolls
As children boys play with cars
As adults women nest
As adults men work

Girls weak
Boys strong
Girls emotional
Boys detached

These are the stereotypes we must break
We must change the world
We must defy all odds
We must be equal

Lauren Villalta

Lauren Villalta was born on August 13,2005. She grew up in the city of South Gate where she now plays soccer for South Gate High School. Some of her hobbies include bracelet-making, listening to music being part of the cross-country, soccer, track and field, and listening to music. In her free time, she likes to go on runs or hangout with friends. Lauren is known to be intelligent, outgoing, honest, hardworking, and committed. In the future, she would like to specialize as a dermatologist.

Breaking the Norms
By Lauren Villalta

Don't do this Don't do that
"That's not very lady-like."
"As a girl you're not supposed to do that."
In today's society we are judged,
We're told not to do things that aren't "girly".

Getting frowned at for doing sports.
People who try to break the norms are considered odd.
Those who don't want to fit in get shamed.
But in my eyes those people are bold.
Daring and courageous .
People who don't care about what others say.
People who challenge society.
People that are able to change things.

To those able to change.
Those who don't care.
Those challenging the norms every step of the way.
Able to do things others can't do.
Doing things only some hope to do.
And for them we should be grateful for.
For those that changed the way we do things.

To all the women playing a "man's sport"
To the male fashion designers.
To the male teachers
And to the male nurses
These are all examples of people breaking the norms.

South Gate High School Girl's Team

People who don't care about norms
And people that changed the way we see things.

Not valued enough in this society.
Not mentioned enough.
Not noticed enough.
But criticized the most.
Not thanked for overstepping boundaries.
And not viewed as a "normal" person.
But in our eyes they are normal and brave.

Yoseline Panduro

Yoseline Panduro is 17 years old and was born in Downey, California on March 21, 2005. She is the only daughter and the youngest out of three siblings which are all boys. She plays club soccer with Cerritos United and high school soccer at South Gate High. Apart from soccer, she enjoys drawing, dancing, and going on runs during her free time. Her future plans include attending a 4 year university to study kinesiology while playing the sport she loves most.

South Gate High School Girl's Team

Blue and Pink
By Yoseline Panduro

Boys wear blue and girls wear pink
That's what society has programmed us to think
I'll stay inside to cook and clean.
While you leave for work to chase your dreams
I wish you well, for that is all I can do.
Since my voice is not as superior as a man's to you
After all, I am pink and you are blue.

All I want is to make him proud
Playing a sport just to see him in the crowd
These clothes bore me and they just don't feel right
I prefer color, I want to shine bright
If I was born this way, is it really my fault?

It feels like a sin, going against everything I was taught
I'm constantly worrying about what they will think
After all, I am blue and you are pink.
The world seems like it has already been set
Two genders: a boy and a girl
A rule that someone out there regrets.
I stand tall regardless.

Refusing to wear the suit and tie
Instead, I'll show up in the pretty prom dress
But when I walk into the room, I can feel all eyes on me
This is who I am
I have no reason to be sorry.

Giselle Bustos

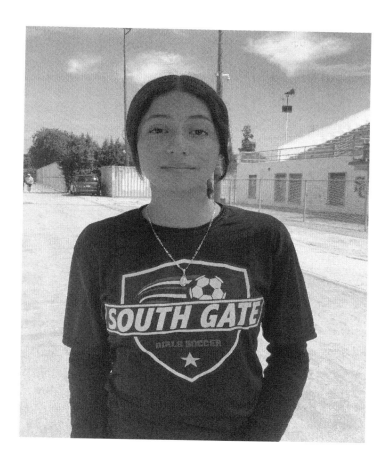

My name is Giselle Bustos. I was born on September 6, 2007 and I am a twin to a brother, who is older than me by very little time. My favorite sport is soccer and my two favorite soccer players are Messi and Cristiano Ronaldo. English is not one of my favorite classes in school but to me it is better than Biology.

Our Meanings of Equality

By Giselle Bustos

Gender Equality has so many meanings to all of us and the perspective of our gender being equal, varies so much for every human being. Gender Equality can be very controversial and it can be debated very often especially depending on the topic that is being discussed. It is a very complex human rights problem that we face everyday even with sports such as with the South Gate High School soccer team. Some of us might settle for certain equalities as a male or as a female and this isn't very fair. Not all the time do we get the rights we deserve or should have because of our gender. If you ask our world what it means to be gender equal, all answers will vary and this is possible based on our biases, opinions, mentality, and so much more.

To begin with, I too have my own definition of what it means to be gender equal. I think that gender equality means a female and a male having equal rights. Gender equality to me means that both genders are allowed to be free without judgment of something being strange for a specific gender to do or practice. Furthermore, gender equality means to do whatever you desire or something specific without your action being judged or seen as something different. Or even something that is not okay for your gender to perform. A specific example that can be judged as something unequal for a specific gender includes playing women's soccer or practicing soccer drills with shorts as a male would, instead of wearing clothing such as leggings as a female and being judged for doing this.

In sports, gender equality could be very unfair and unequal because people stereotype certain sports to be for a specific gender. This includes soccer because it is very often that females are judged for playing soccer. Sometimes people think that soccer is a sport only for males and we are judged for playing as females or empowered women on a soccer field. With soccer I have noticed that a lot of schools focus on boys soccer and some people give all their attention to soccer games when boys play or when they train for a game. I have noticed multiple times in other schools that boys soccer will get beautiful uniforms and nicer equipment while girls soccer will get equipment or tools that the boys might have previously used or just in general cheaper equipment. This is not very gender equal and it relates back to our gender because if it was boys soccer that needed equipment, people are quick to buy it while for females, there is always an excuse.

In addition, to elaborate over gender equality, I think that being gender equal includes sharing the same opportunities and even resources as a female or a male. In this world, it is sad to state but it is very common that females get treated very differently than males. Women are often known as weaker than a male, less intelligent, or even not capable of a lot just because of our gender. Apart from sports such as soccer, gender inequalities are very uncommon everywhere. I see people being judged or treated differently because of their gender in jobs, education, and in the media as well. Sometimes when I play soccer I feel like I am being judged because I am a female playing a sport that is often thought to be for males only. Growing up in a hispanic household I have often understood that some things may or may not be for females or for males. This includes colors or certain clothes being placed for a certain gender such as pink or blue.

Everyone has their own definition of gender equality such as the definition that I have concluded.I have learned a lot about gender equality in soccer as someone who plays girls soccer on a high school team. This includes sharing equal opportunities and privileges in sports, jobs, and so much more all over the world. Overall, I think that gender equality means to have equal opportunities and rights no matter your gender. We have so many definitions of gender equality and I believe it means to be equal no matter your gender.

Denise Ramirez

My name is Denise Ramirez and I am 17 years old and I am currently a Senior at South Gate High School. I live with my two parents and 2 older brothers. I've been playing soccer for 7 years and I'm glad to say I'm ending my high school soccer experience on a great note. This is something I worked hard on since I first joined this program, and I'm glad I had the opportunity to win a CIF championship with a great group of powerful young ladies.

South Gate High School Girl's Team

Mujeres Poderosas- Powerful Women
By Denise Ramirez

2022, I believe, was a discovery year for me. It was a year of self acceptance. I don't necessarily believe I follow gender norms because I believe there shouldn't be any. I believe people should be able to wear whatever they desire and what they feel the most comfortable in, the typical pink for girls, blue for boys shouldn't even be a thing nowadays anyone should be able to express themselves the way they like with whatever color they desire. This world is a challenging place to live in and you will always have someone judging your every move. In this world I believe many people set up their own expectations that they believe others should follow and that's not the case. Everyone has the right to their own opinion and believe what is right or wrong for themselves but they should never discriminate/disrespect what others believe.

Coming from a very religious and old fashion family background, I grew up with the idea in my head that a color had a gender, which now I think is completely wrong, a person should be able to express themselves with whichever color they desire. Being part of the LGBTQ community and in a very religious and old fashion family is a challenge.

This new generation has grown up in a more exposed and open minded community which I believe has helped many people around the world finally be their true selves which was not the case for many people 25 years ago, Which is the reason why people back then were most close minded and grew up with the idea that only women wear dresses or only mean wear suits.

Sadly, in this world people still get treated differently and there are still some people that hide their true identity because they are afraid of being judged or hurt by others. Often people feel "threatened" by people that decide to break gender norms.

They believe people who dress as they desire are a danger to society. I truly don't understand why people think this way, no one is being harmed and no one is being forced to do anything they don't want. Often these ideas get put into young children's minds when in reality they are still too young to understand true identities and genders.

I believe that my group of friends don't adhere to the gender norms, I believe we are all very careless of what others will say and other may think when we wear caps and baggy clothes with many consider "boy clothes", for example something i've been experiencing this past couple weeks is the decision of whether I choose to wear a dress to prom or a tuxedo,and what many would believe the right thing to do is to wear a dress.I believe an article of clothing shouldn't have a gender and I should choose what I feel most comfortable in. Coming from an old fashion family it is very hard to convince them to let me wear a tuxedo. Growing up as their only little girl and being their only daughter they obviously want to see their little girl dress up one last time to go to prom. Walking into a store can already feel intimidating, now walking into a store as a female and asking to look for a tux that can be a bit nerve wracking because you don't know how that person will react, you don't know if they will treat you with the say respect as they treated client that is "following the gender role norms."

As expressed, I believe there is still work to be done but we are on the right track. It's just a matter of time and getting those people that are still close minded to understand that expressing your true identity is no threat. People should feel welcomed and accepted for who they are.

Yoseline Martínez

My name is Yoseline Martinez. I am 15 years old and I live in the city of South Gate. I attend South Gate High School and play for the soccer team. I am the J.V. Captain of the soccer team and love to play and interact with my teammates. I also love and enjoy being part of a program called AVID at school. I like being involved with my school and interacting with my teachers.

For Boys and For Girls Only
Por: Yoseline Martínez

Many of us have the idea that some things are "for girls only" and some things "for boys only" but crazy as it sounds there is no such thing as that. We have the idea of that because of where we come from. Most of us come from immigrant parents that raised us to think that way because they were raised that way. But times have changed where people think differently about stuff like this topic including me. I am a 15 year old girl raised by immigrant parents and have an immigrant family that thinks there's certain things for each gender. Let me tell you about my experience.

One day I was playing basketball with my boy cousins outside our house. We were of course enjoying playing because we were kids and didn't think there was such a thing called "girl things and boy things". After a while of playing with my cousins, my grandma came outside and saw me playing with them. I remember she pulled me aside and told me why am I playing with my cousins if they're boys. Me being small and unconnected didn't know what she was talking about. I still remember till this day when she told me that " I am supposed to be playing with dolls and not basketball because that was a boy thing and not a girl thing to do". That was very heartful to hear from my grandma because I was young. As hurtful as it was, I didn't let it get to me. I continued playing but what my grandma said was still sitting in the back of my head. I told myself that wasn't true and every toy in the world and sport is for both boys and girls.

My sister, who is 12 year old, is going through changes as she progresses into a teenager. The changes that she is going through are not very similar to the changes I went through when I was becoming a teenager. You would expect her to start experimenting with makeup and "girly things" girls do, but she is the opposite. She dresses differently, she wears baggy clothes, likes to go out with friends, and doesn't get ready as often. My mom has told her many times that she isn't supposed to wear baggy clothes and not get ready many times because those are things boys do. In the beginning my mom didn't understand or like the way she was dressing, but as time passed I supported my sister and helped my mom understand because my sister dresses a certain way and acts differently doesn't mean anything that a girl could be or what a girl should do. My mom was hesitant at first but then understood that my sister likes doing her things differently. I was glad that I was able to help change my mom's thinking and most importantly help my sister. That's how I would want to change my whole family's view of things.

Once I got to high school, I wanted to try something new and find out who I am. Many people join clubs, sports, and try new hobbies they might like. I wanted to try something new, something way out of my comfort zone, and something I've never seen myself doing. I joined soccer, at first it was hard because I was doing something I wasn't used to but now I've found my love for the sport and love the people I'm surrounded by and the coaches. When I broke the news to my family that I've decided to join soccer, some of them found it really cool and were happy for me and some had a different opinion about it. My grandma and my aunts told me that why didn't I join something else that "girls do" and not a "boy thing". Another really shocking thing they told me, inside of doing things that are not going to help me with my future, I should be learning how to cook and clean. That really hurts my feelings especially coming from my own family and blood. That doesn't stop me though, I won't let their words and thoughts get to me. From that day on I've learned to not listen to other people and continue to do what I love doing.

Everyone should go ahead and do what they love even if it has gender labels according to society. Don't let the idea that there are certain things that for girls and others that are for boys get to you. Every toy in the world, every sport in the world, and every clothing is for everybody. It doesn't matter what gender you are or race you are. Everybody should be free to do what they want and love. Although many of us are raised by immigrant parents or those that will bring up and speak to you about gender roles understand that times are changing, not everything that they did in past time is going to work now or should be like that today. Change is always good, it's for the best for the new generations and our kids, for them to be comfortable with the things that they like and do no matter if others are not okay with them. Be brave, be unique, and most of all, be happy with whom you are.

Hector Huizar

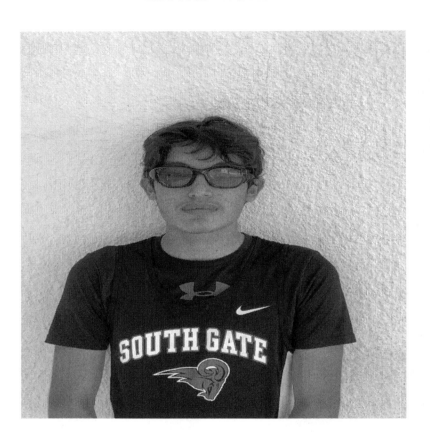

My name is Hector Huizar. I am a senior at South Gate High School and I enjoy doing sports. I do sports such as Cross Country, Track and Field, and Boxing. I also sometimes like to write for fun and read books. My favorite book I've read is the story of Beowulf.

Mamá, Mujer Poderosa

By Hector Huizar

Todos la llaman mujer o señora,
pero yo la llamo mamá.
Maravillosa creada por Dios
Única en mi vida.

Jamás se rinde ante nada.
Es la que jamás abandona.
Rie aunque algunas veces por dentro está destrozada.
Y nunca me cambiaría por nada.

Siempre cuento con ella.
Es más fuerte de lo que yo puedo imaginar.
Ella busca solución al más mínimo problema.
Mi mamá es mi heroína porque es la mujer más fuerte que
conozco.

Ella es mi inspiración para luchar hasta lograr mi objetivo.

Sebastiana

Hola, mi nombre es Sebastiana y tengo 17 años. Soy de Guatemala y me gusta hacer deporte todos los días. Vengo con un propósito a este país, el salir adelante con mis padres y espero que algún día todos mis sueños se me hagan realidad. Me siento muy feliz por estar en este país, nunca me iba a imaginar estar en un lugar muy maravilloso. Le doy gracias a Dios por darme una oportunidad de conocer a mi mamá y a mis hermanos los amo familia.

Amistad en versos

By Sebastiana

La amistad es una relación que todos tenemos en estos días. Oré por ti y me puse a recordar a mis amistades más preciosas.

Soy una persona muy feliz porque tengo más amigas de lo que me imaginaba, eso me hace feliz y me lo demuestran con honestidad, confianza, apoyo y es por eso que una verdadera amistad es muy difícil de conseguir y de confiar, siempre hay que tener una amistad con tu familia.

Algunas veces en la vida encuentras una amistad muy especial para ti y alguien que entra en tu vida para cambiarte por completo todo de ti y te hace reír y te hace ver que en el mundo existen cosas muy hermosas aunque el mundo te lleve a un camino distinto.

Tus amistades te recordarán con mucho cariño y tus recuerdos siempre te acompañarán hasta el fin del mundo.

Un amigo te enseña cosas buenas que tú nunca has aprendido en la vida, el amigo sabe muchas cosas de ti y a pesar de todo ellos te quieren como un hermano que tú eres para ello, el amigo que te quiere te acepta tal y como tu eres y siempre te apoyara en las buenas y en las malas y siempre van a estar contigo sin importarle como tu eres con ellos ya que una amistad eterna no tiene fin.

Le doy gracias a Dios que me haya puesto personas maravillosas a mi lado, porque la amistad es muy linda y es para todo la vida y lo más importante es saber que siempre puedes contar con un verdadero amigo que te escucha y te ofrece su hombro para poder ver la vida de otra manera.

La vida te da muchas oportunidades y hay que aprovecharla y siempre y hay que pedirle a Dios que nos cuide y nos proteja y que siempre las personas que queremos estemos juntos para toda la vida.

Quiero agradecerle a una persona muy especial para mi que me ha brindado una amistad muy bonita, se que puedo contar contigo en momento difícil y de angustia y también compartir mis alegría. Mamá eres la más bella del mundo, eres la luz de mi vida, eres mi amor profundo, la que me trajo en este mundo. Gracias por darme tus palabras sinceras y tu amor incondicional y le pido a Dios que siempre te cuide mamá.

KICKING
Through Fields of Hope

INDEX

Made in the USA
Columbia, SC
30 June 2022

62512851R00065